T0084178

SCHIRMER'S LIBRARY
OF MUSICAL CLASSICS

WOLFGANG AMADEUS MOZART

Nineteen Sonatas
For the Piano

(ENGLISH AND SPANISH)

Revised and Edited by
RICHARD EPSTEIN

With a Biographical Sketch of the Composer by
PHILIP HALE

Book I (Nos. 1-10) — Library Vol. 1305

➤ Book II (Nos. 11-19) — Library Vol. 1306

Complete — Library Vol. 1304

Accompaniments for Second Piano by
Edvard Grieg, for Nos. 3, 4, 5 and 18,
may be found in
Library Vols. 1440-1-2-3 respectively

G. SCHIRMER, Inc.

DISTRIBUTED BY

HAL•LEONARD®
CORPORATION
7777 W. BLUEMOUND RD. P.O. BOX 13819 MILWAUKEE, WI 53213

Copyright, 1918, by G. Schirmer, Inc.
Printed in the U. S. A.

Thematic Index
Índice Temático

Book I
Libro I

Book II
Libro II

The identifying numbers in brackets [ ] are those that appear in the 3rd edition
of Köchel's *Mozart-Verzeichnis* (1937). The identifying numbers in parentheses ( )
are those that appear in previous editions of Köchel's *Verzeichnis*.

Les números que aparecen en paréntesis angulares [ ] son los que corresponden a la 3a edición
del *Mozart-Verzeichnis* de Köchel (1937). Les números que aparecen en paréntesis ( ) son los
que corresponden a las ediciones previas del *Verzeichnis* de Köchel.

Sonata XI

Edited, revised and fingered by
Richard Epstein

Abbreviations: P. T., Principal Theme; S. T., Secondary Theme; M. T., Middle Theme; Ep., Episode.

Abreviaciones: T. P., Tema Principal; T. S., Tema Segundo; T. M., Tema Medio; Ep., Episodio.

Allegro moderato (♩ = 126)

Copyright, 1918, by G. Schirmer, Inc.
Printed in the U. S. A.

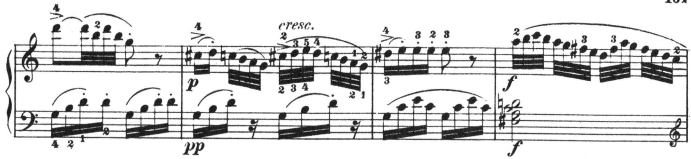

a)

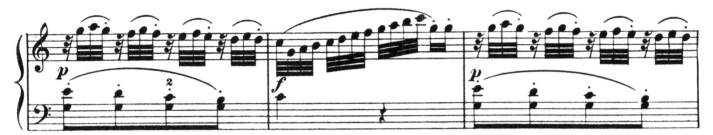

Close I
1ª Coda

Close II
2ª Coda

Coda
Coda

178

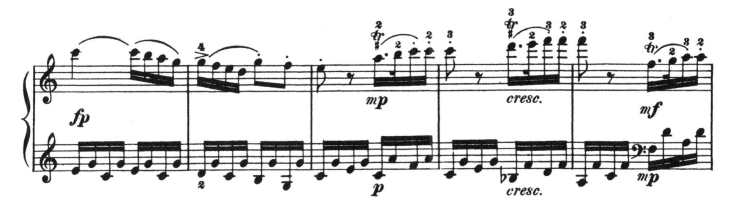

Sonata XII

Edited, revised and fingered by
Richard Epstein

Abbreviations: P.T., Principal Theme; S.T., Secondary Theme; D., Development; T., Transition; R., Return; Ep., Episode.

Abreviaciones: T.P., Tema Principal; T.S., Tema Segundo; D., Desarrollo; T., Transición; R., Retorno; Ep., Episodio.

Copyright, 1918, by G. Schirmer, Inc.

Close
Coda

Ped. ✳ Ped. ✳

Close
1ª Coda

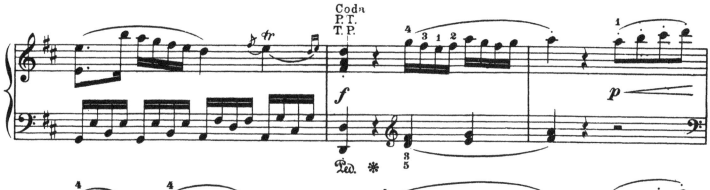

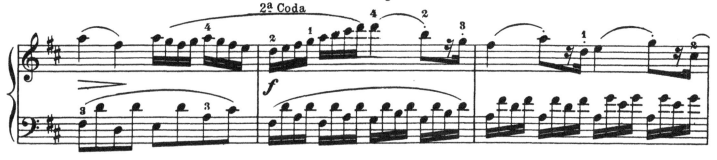

Andante con espressione (♪=96)

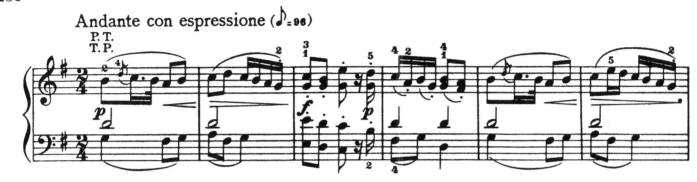

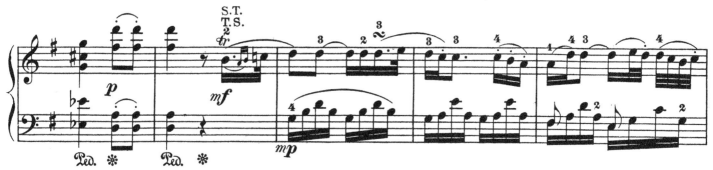

Close
Coda

a)

Rondo

Allegro (♩. = 96)

a)

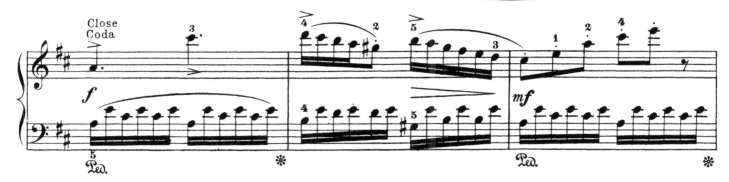

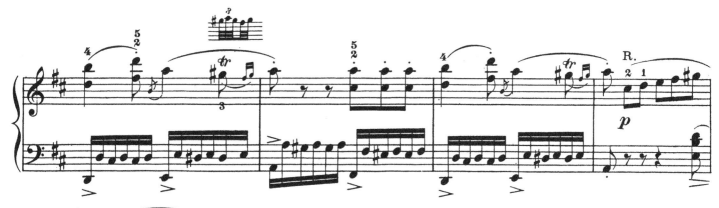

Ep.

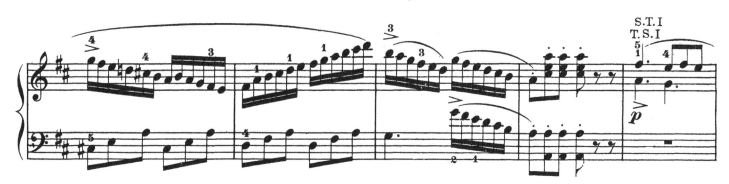

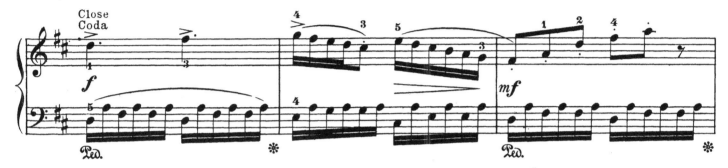

Close
Coda

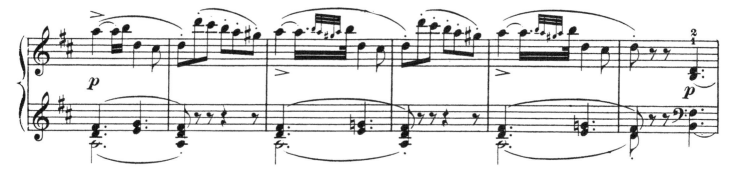

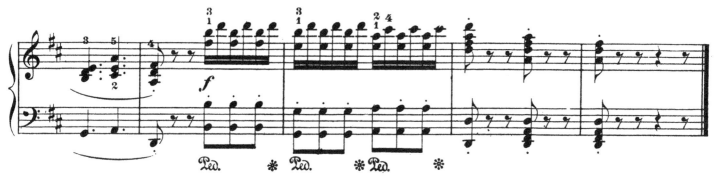

Sonata XIII

Edited, revised and fingered by
Richard Epstein

Abbreviations: P. T., Principal Theme; S. T., Secondary Theme; M. T., Middle Theme. | Abreviaciones: T. P., Tema Principal; T. S., Tema Segundo; T. M., Tema Medio.

Copyright, 1918, by G. Schirmer, Inc.

Printed in the U. S. A.

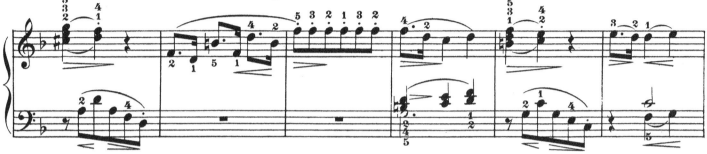

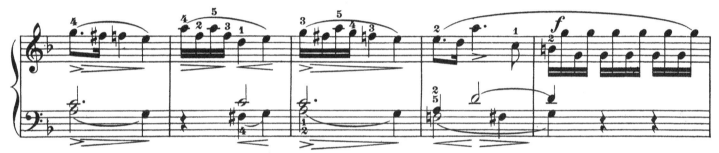

a)

Close
Coda

M.T.
T.M.

a)   b)

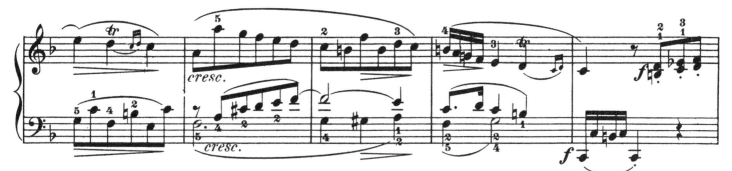

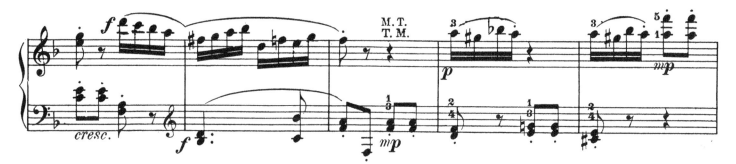

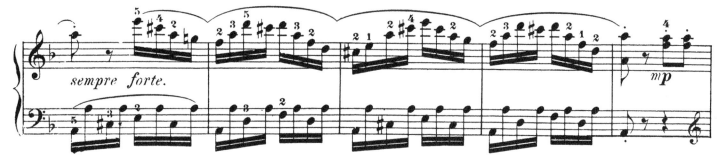

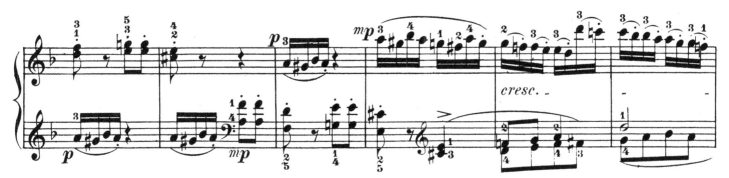

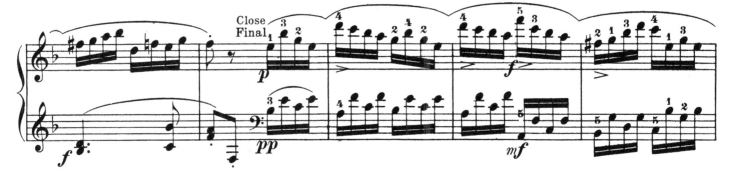

Sonata XIV

Edited, revised and fingered by
Richard Epstein

Abbreviations: P.T., Principal Theme; S.T., Secondary Theme; D., Development; Ep., Episode; M.T., Middle Theme; R., Return.

Abreviaciones: T.P., Tema Principal; T.S., Tema Segundo; D., Desarrollo; Ep., Episodio; T.M., Tema Medio; R., Retorno.

Allegro maestoso (♩ = 116)

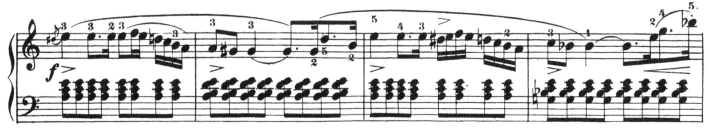

Copyright, 1918, by G. Schirmer, Inc.

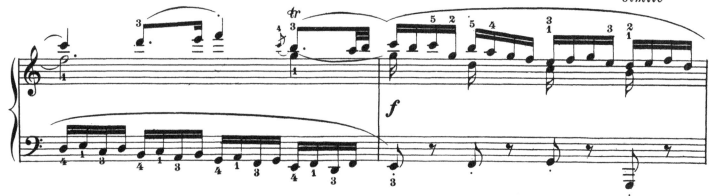

a)  b)

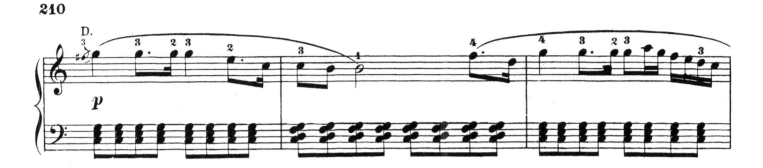

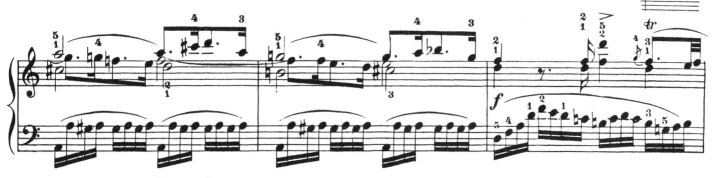

Andante cantabile con espressione ($\downarrow$=96)

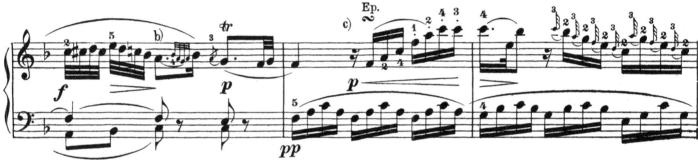

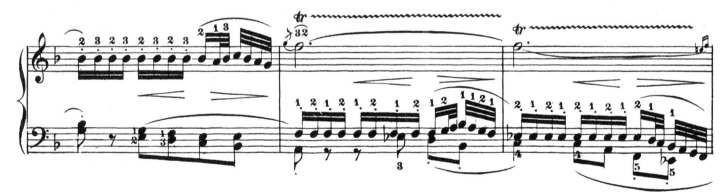

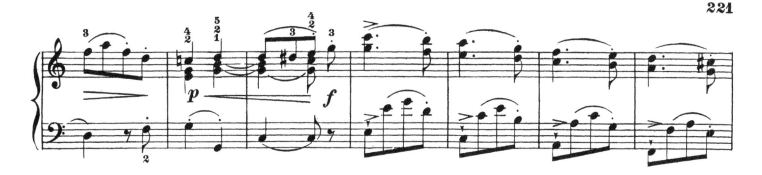

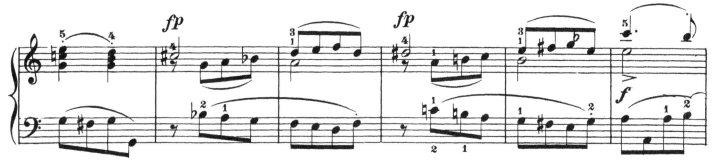

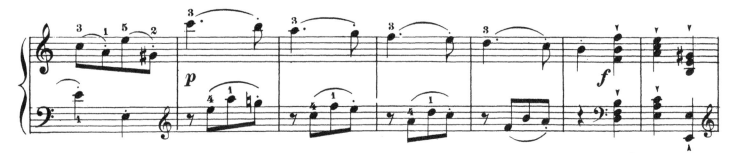

Close
Final

Sonata XV

Edited, revised and fingered by
Richard Epstein

Abbreviations: P.T., Principal Theme; S.T., Secondary Theme; D., Development; R., Return.

Abreviaciones: T.P., Tema Principal; T.S., Tema Segundo; D., Desarrollo; R., Retorno.

Allegro ($\bullet$ = 84)

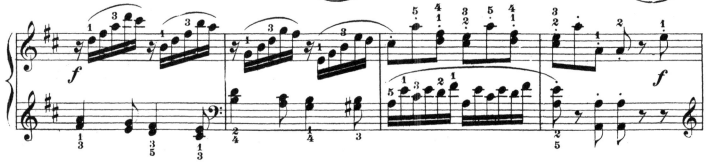

Copyright, 1918, by G. Schirmer, Inc.

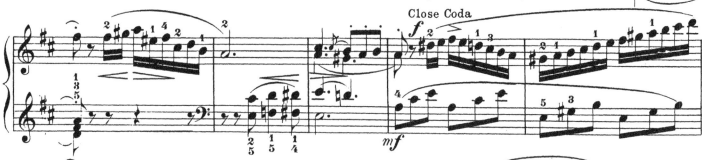

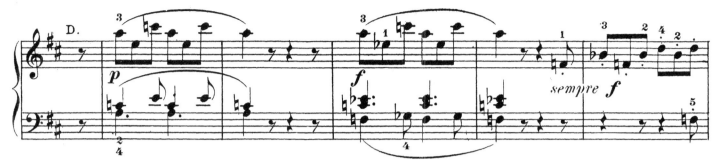

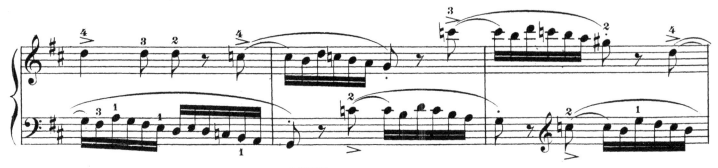

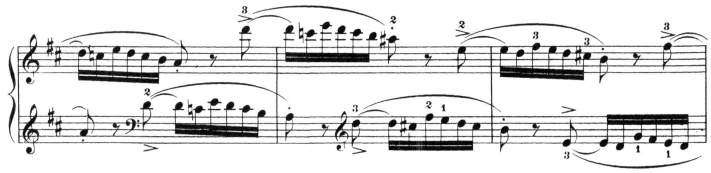

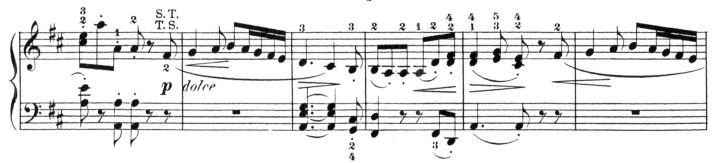

Adagio (♩= 96)

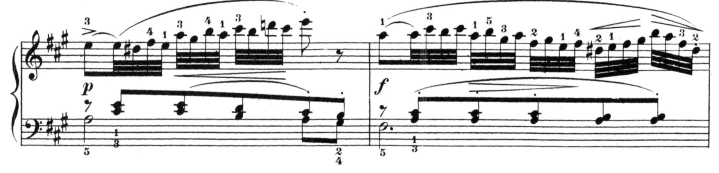

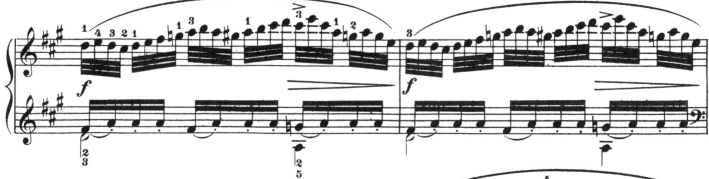

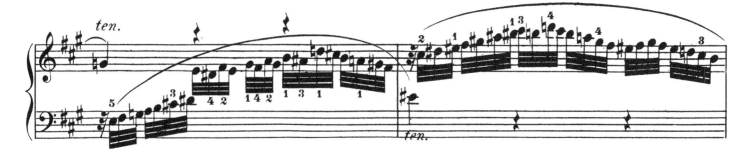

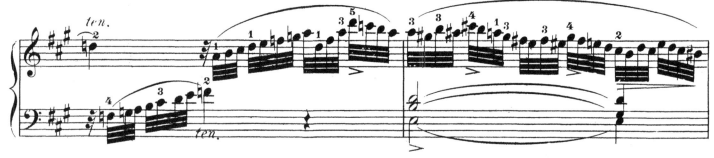

a)

236
Allegretto (♩ = 88)

Close Final

Sonata XVI

Edited, revised and fingered by
Richard Epstein

Abbreviations: P. T., Principal Theme; S. T., Secondary Theme.

Abreviaciones: T. P., Tema Principal; T. S., Tema Segundo.

Tema
Andante grazioso (♪=120)

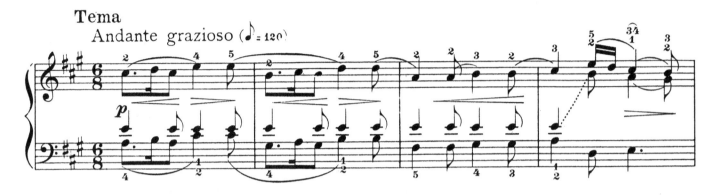

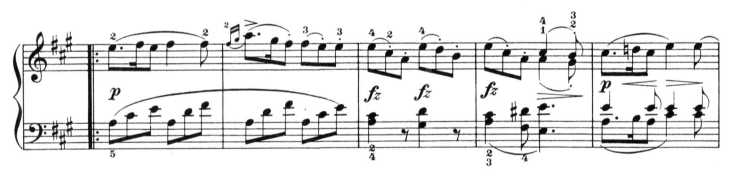

Var. I

Copyright, 1918, by G. Schirmer, Inc.

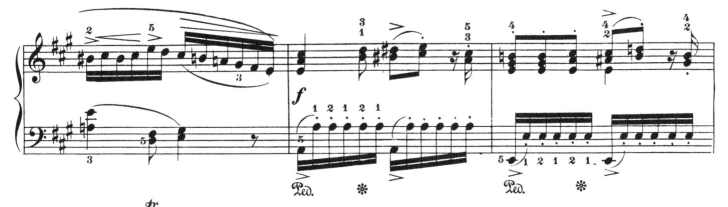

Var. II

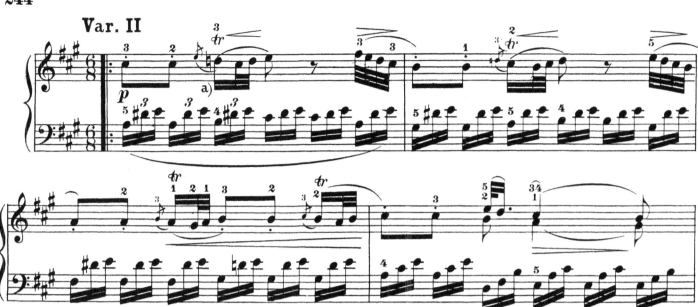

Var. III (♪ = 112)

Minore

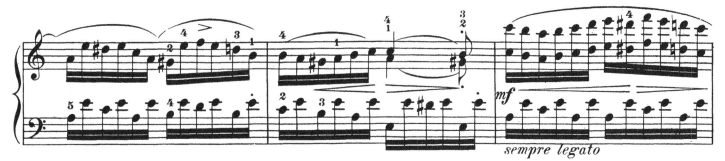

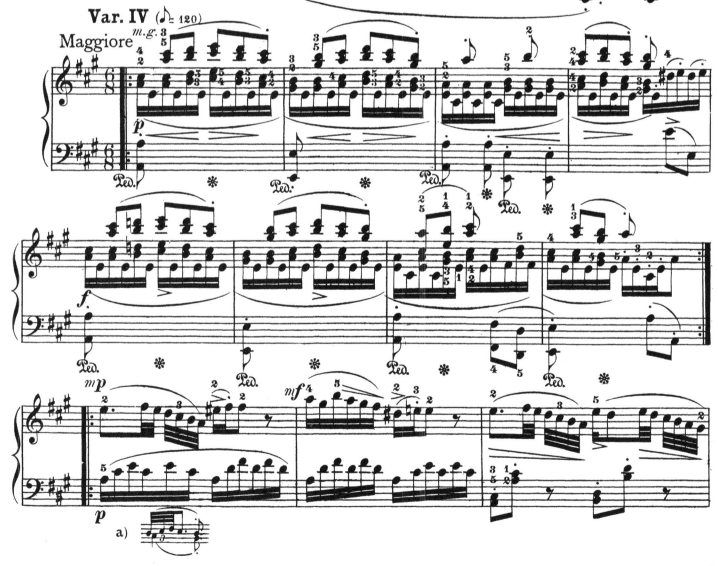

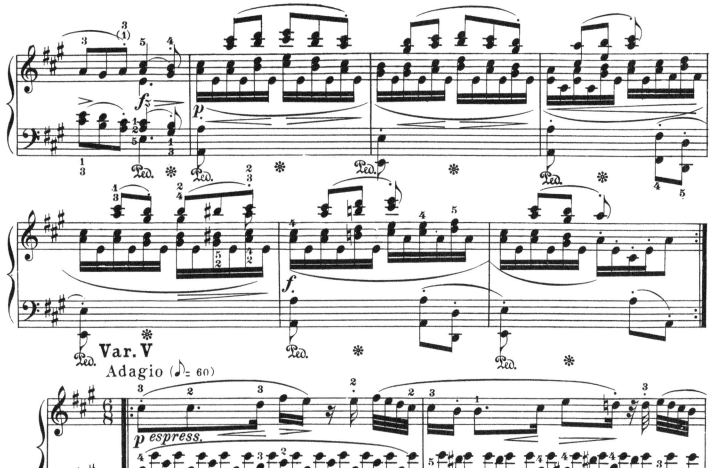

Var. V

Adagio (♪ = 60)

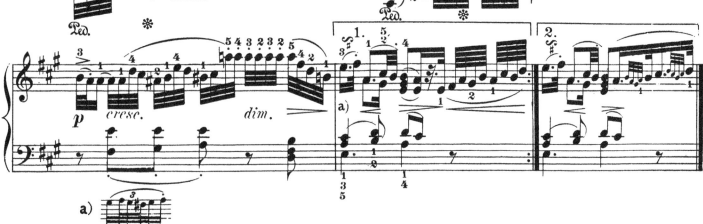

a)

Var. VI

Allegro (♩ = 116)

a) The C sharp must enter with the bass note of the left hand.

a) El Do sostenido debe atacarse al mismo tiempo que la primera nota del arpegio de la mano izquierda.

Menuetto (♩ = 116)

Trio

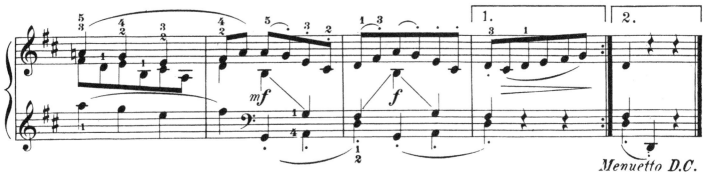

Menuetto D.C.

Alla turca

Allegretto (♩ = 126)

Rondo

W. A. MOZART

a)

b) Play the first A in the bass with the C sharp in the right hand.

b) Tóquese el Do♯ del acompañamiento con la mano derecha.

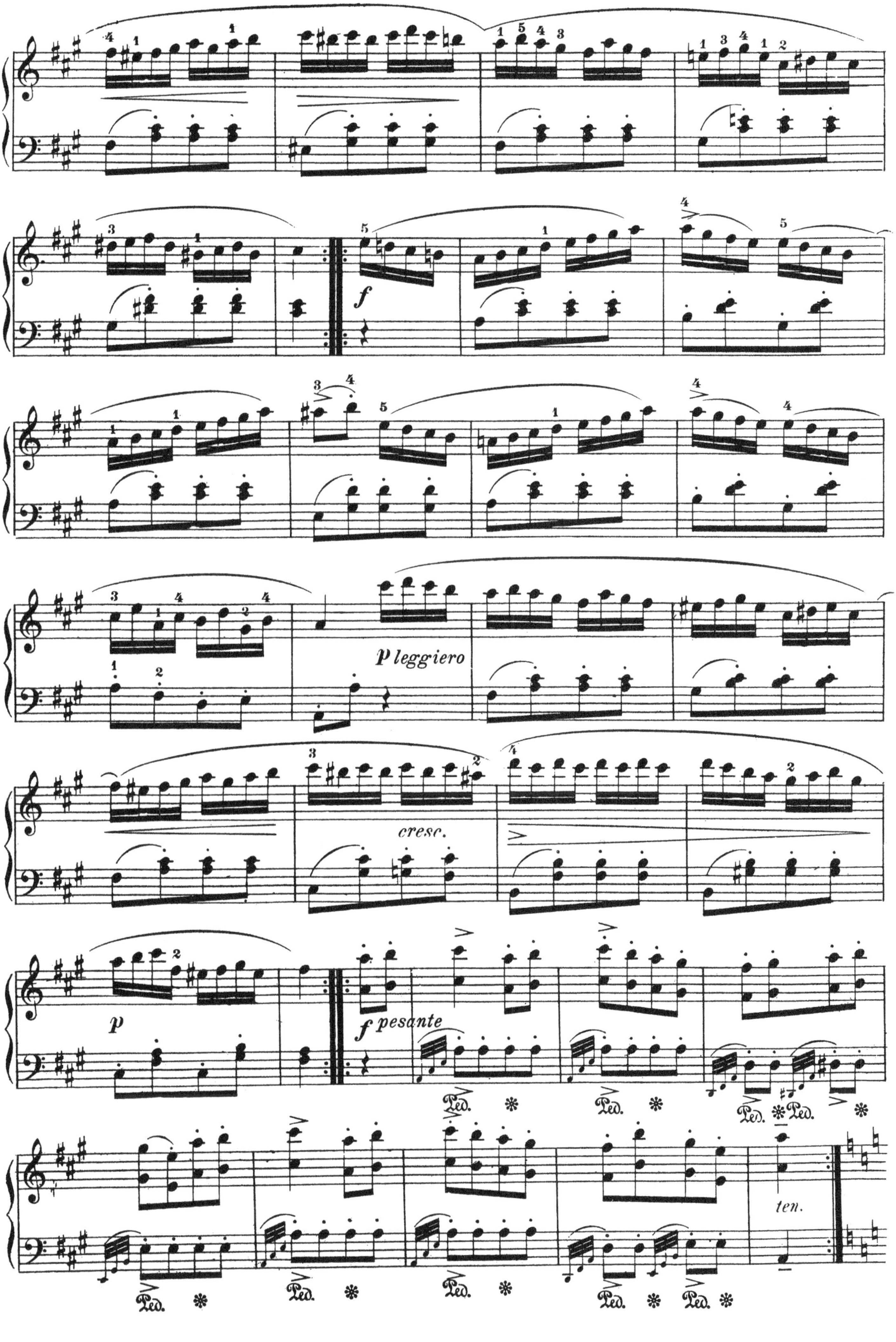
p leggiero
cresc.
p
f pesante
Ped.
ten.

a) Play the four notes in either hand simultaneously.

a) Tóquense las cuatro notas simultáneamente con las dos manos.

b)

Edited, revised and fingered by
Richard Epstein

Sonata XVII
[K. 189⁹ (formerly 282)]

Abbreviations: P.T., Principal Theme; S.T., Secondary Theme; T., Transition; D., Development.

Abreviaciones: T.P., Tema Principal; T.S., Tema Segundo; T., Transición; D., Desarrollo.

Adagio

Copyright, 1918, by G. Schirmer, Inc.

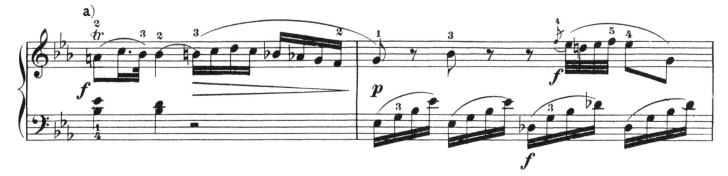

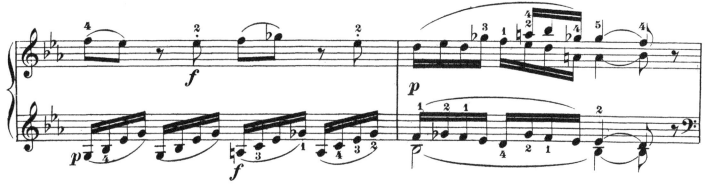

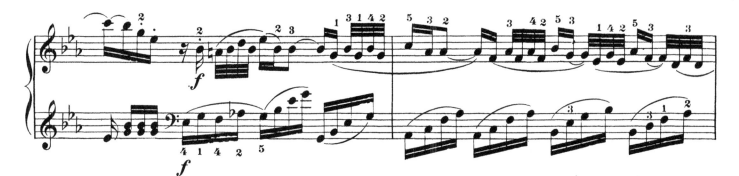

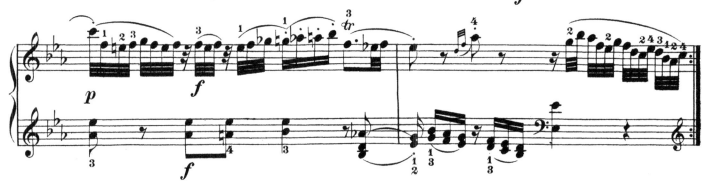

Coda

a)

Menuetto I

Menuetto II

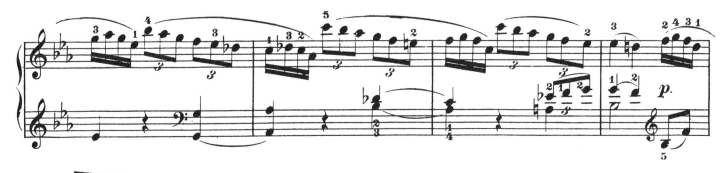

a)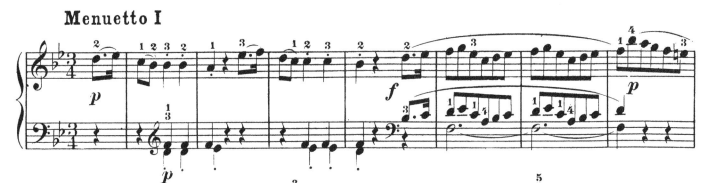

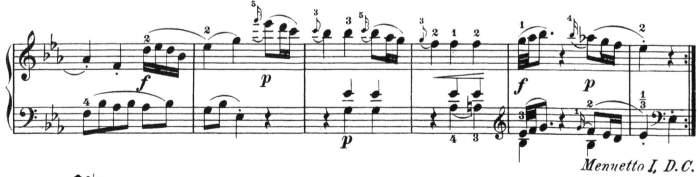

Menuetto I, D.C.

a) b)

Allegro

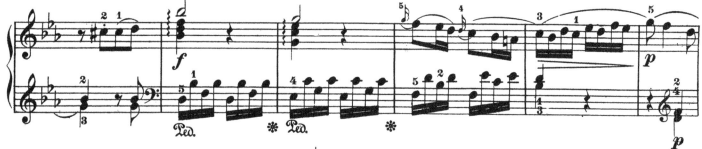

a) b) c)

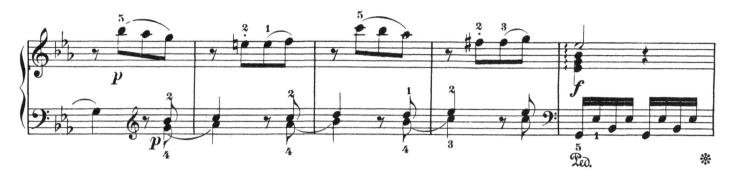

Close
Coda

Fantasia and Sonata XVIII*
Fantasia y Sonata

*Edited, revised and fingered by
Richard Epstein*

W. A. MOZART

Fantasia
Adagio (♩ = 76)

*An accompaniment for Second Piano by Edvard Grieg may be found in Schirmer's Library, Vol. 1443.

Copyright, 1918, by G. Schirmer, Inc.

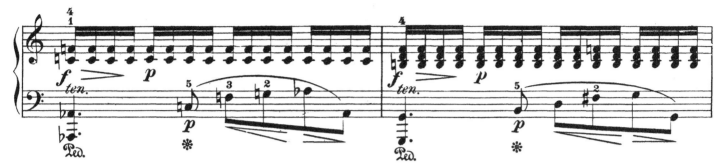

a) [music example]

b) The 2nd, 4th, 6th, and 8th notes in this measure may be played with the left hand.

b) La 2ª, 4ª, 6ª y 8ª nota en este compás se pueden tocar con la mano izquierda.

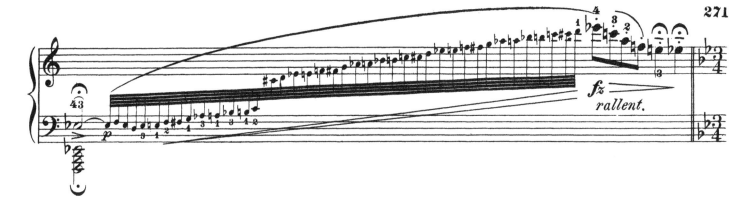

Più allegro (♩. = 66)

il basso marcato

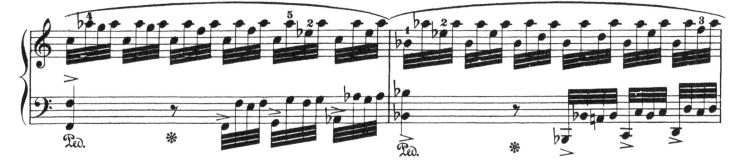

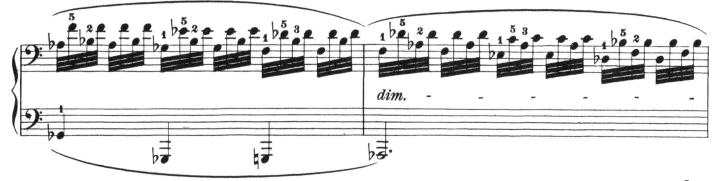

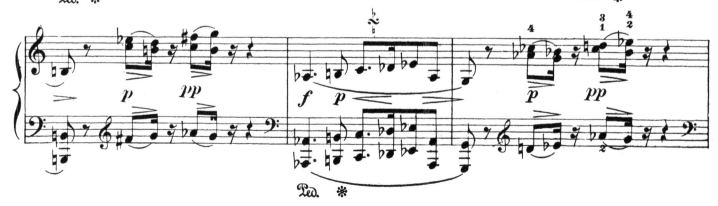

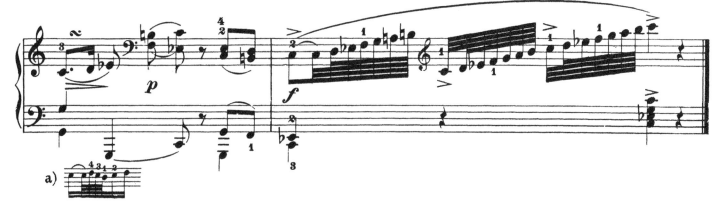

Abbreviations: P.T., Principal Theme; Ep., Episode; S.T., Secondary Theme; T., Transition; D., Development; R., Return.

Abreviaciones: T.P., Tema Principal; Ep., Episodio; T.S., Tema Segundo; T., Transición; D. Desarrollo; R., Retorno.

a) The 2nd, 4th and 6th notes, etc., in this passage may be played with the right hand.

a) Las notas 2ª, 4ª, 6ª, etc., de este pasaje pueden tocarse con la mano derecha.

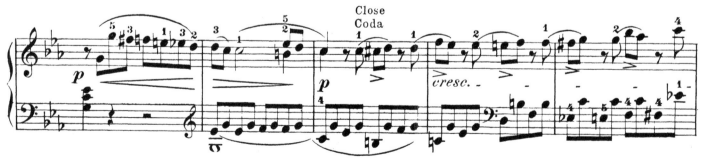

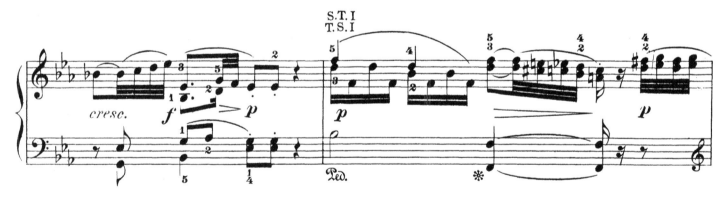

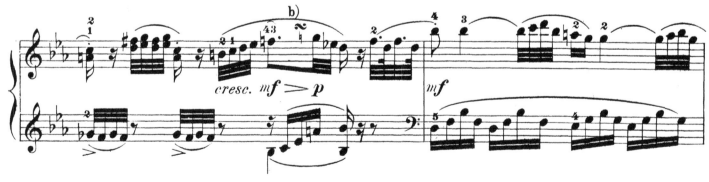

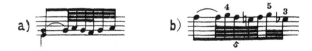

S.T. II
T.S. II

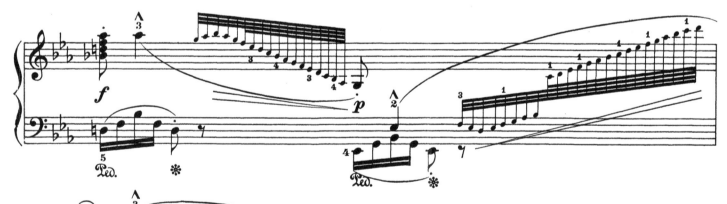

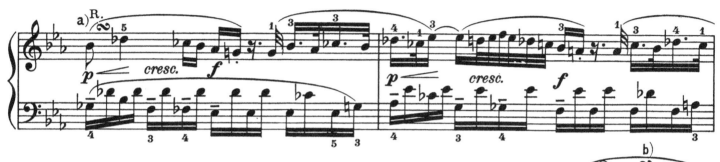

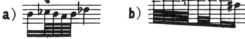

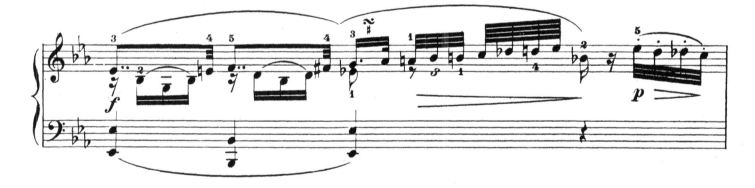

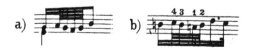

Close I
Final I

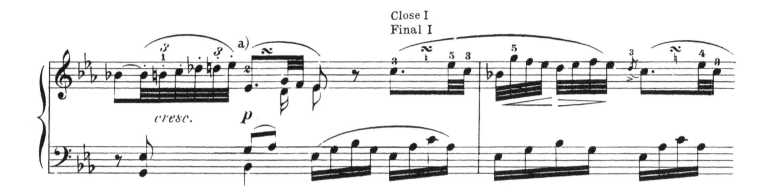

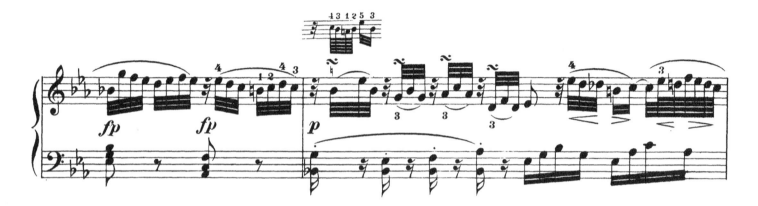

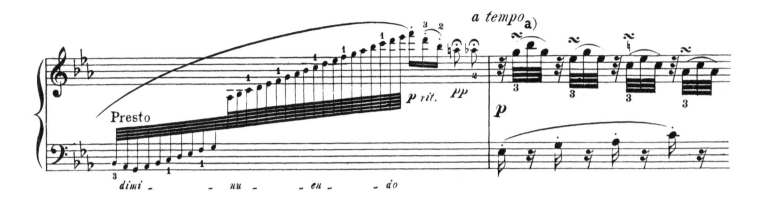

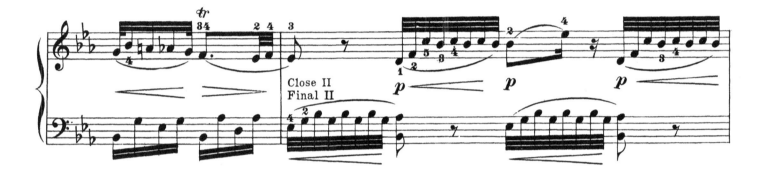

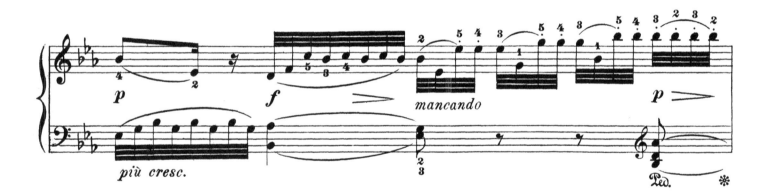

Allegro assai (♩.=66)

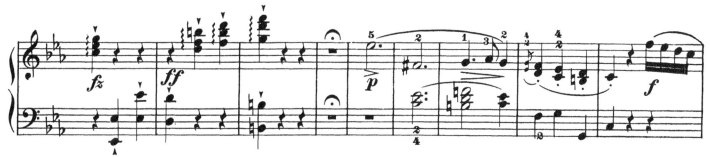

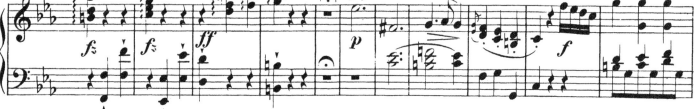

Sonata XIX

Edited, revised and fingered by
Richard Epstein

Abbreviations: P. T., Principal Theme; S. T., Secondary Theme: D., Development; Th., Theme; Var., Variation; Ep., Episode; R., Return; T., Transition.

Abreviaciones: T. P., Tema Principal; T. S., Tema Segundo; D., Desarrollo; Ta., Tema; Var., Variación; Ep., Episodio; R., Retorno; T., Transición.

Copyright, 1918, by G. Schirmer, Inc.
Printed in the U. S. A.

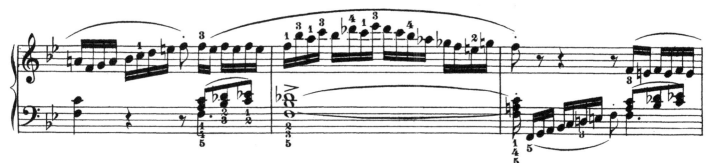

Andante (♩ = 76)

Var. I

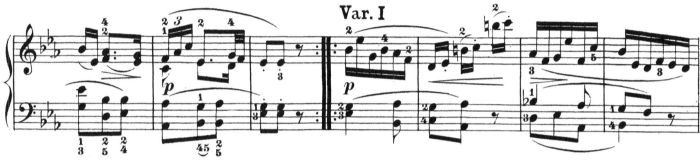

Var. II

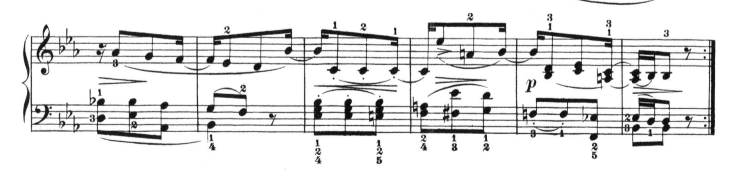

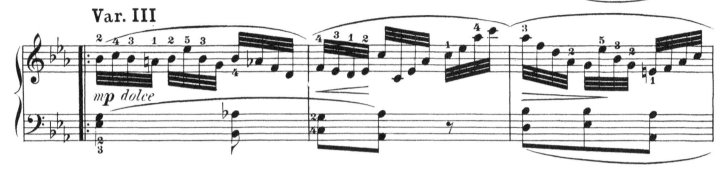

Var. III

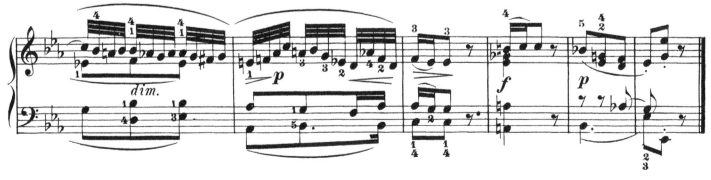

Menuetto

Allegretto (♩=144)

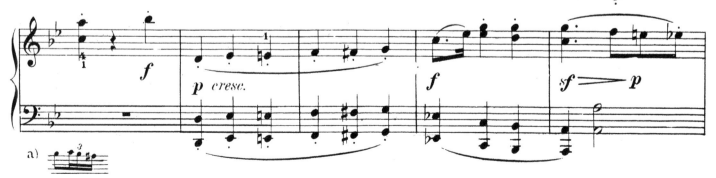

a)

Trio

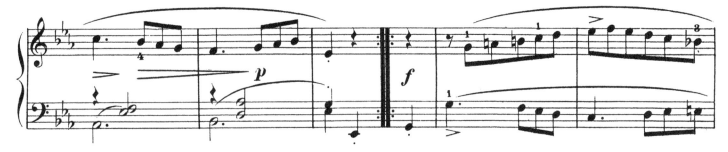

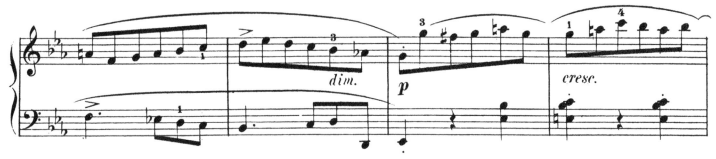

Menuetto D. C.

a)

Rondo

Allegro (♩.= 100)

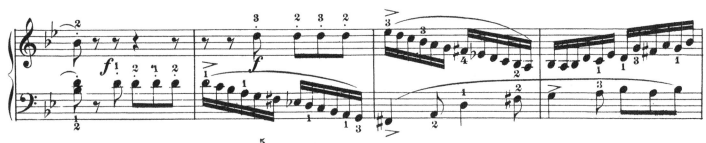

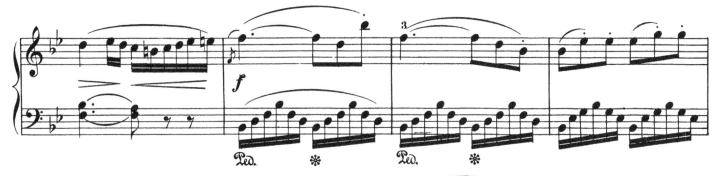

Tempo Iº

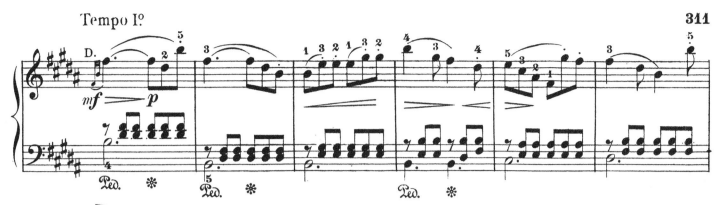

Tempo Iº

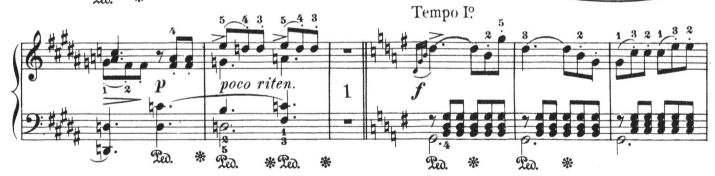